364.609

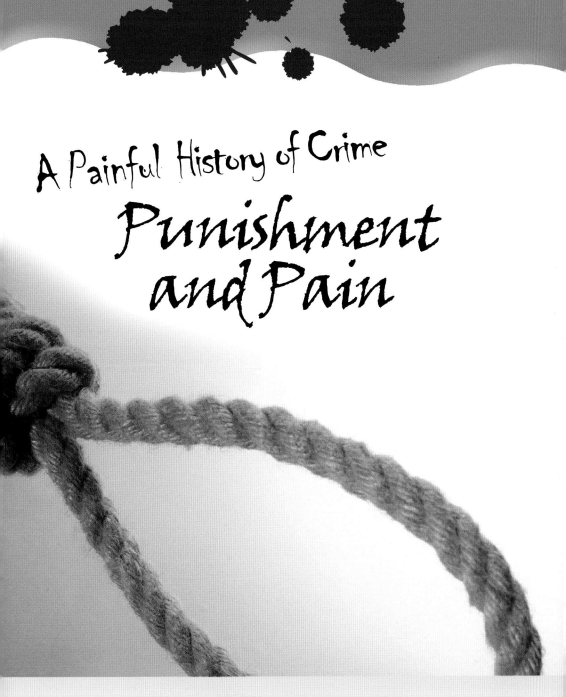

A Painful History of Crime

Punishment and Pain

John Townsend

www.raintreepublishers.co.uk

Visit our website to find out more information about **Raintree** books.

To order:
☎ Phone 44 (0) 1865 888113
🖹 Send a fax to 44 (0) 1865 314091
🖥 Visit the Raintree bookshop at **www.raintreepublishers.co.uk**
to browse our catalogue and order online.

First published in Great Britain by Raintree,
Halley Court, Jordan Hill, Oxford OX2 8EJ,
part of Harcourt Education.
Raintree is a registered trademark
of Harcourt Education Ltd.

Editorial: Melanie Copland
and Kate Buckingham
Design: Lucy Owen
and Bridge Creative Services Ltd
Picture Research: Hannah Taylor
and Ginny Stroud-Lewis
Production: Duncan Gilbert

Originated by Chroma Graphics (Overseas) Pte. Ltd
Printed and bound in China by South China
Printing Company

ISBN 1 844 21388 9
09 08 07 06 05
10 9 8 7 6 5 4 3 2 1

**British Library Cataloguing in
Publication Data**
Townsend, John
Punishment and pain – (A Painful History
of Crime)
364.6'09
A full catalogue record for this book is available
from the British Library.

Acknowledgements
Art Directors **29** (Victor Watts), Colonial
Williamsburg Collection pp **5b**, **17**, **23**, Corbis
pp **1**, **24** (Royalty Free), **40-41** (Charles O'Rear),
5m, **8**, **14**, **16**, **18r**, **21**, **22**, **27**, **32-33**
(Bettman), **28-29** (Gianni Dagli Orti), **34** (Mark
Jenkinson), DKImages **38**, Getty Images pp **42-
43**; **5t**, **18l**, **11b**, **24-25**, **28**, **31**, **30**, **35**, **42**
(Hulton Archive), **41** (Image Source), **15**
(Photodisc), Mary Evans Picture Library pp **4-5**,
4, **6**, **7**, **9**, **11t**, **12-13**, **19**, **20t**, **32**; **33**
(Graystone Bird, Bath), Rex Features pp **39**, **40**,
The Bridgeman Art Library pp **10** (Lambeth
Palace Library, London, UK), **20** (Pushkin
Museum, Moscow, Russia), The Kobal Collection
pp **22-23** (MGM), **36** (Paramount), **26-27**
(Samuel Bronston), **37** (United Artists), The
Library of Congress **12**.

Cover photograph of execution chair
reproduced with permission of Corbis/Bettman.

Contents

Any words appearing in the text in bold,
like this, are explained in the glossary. You can
also look out for them in the Word bank box at
the bottom of each page.

Do as you are told!

Most people believe that doing wrong usually deserves some sort of penalty. They think this shows which ways of behaving are good and which are bad. If people suffer for committing a crime, perhaps they will never do it again. Through history, views about right and wrong, as well as punishment, have changed a lot.

❝If you do not behave, you will be punished!❞

Many children have grown up hearing these words. Being punished is the price we pay for doing wrong.

If you break the rules of a game, you usually get some sort of **penalty**. If you break the laws of the land, you usually get punished. In some places that might mean you:

- pay a fine
- get locked in prison
- do hard work
- are made to feel shame in front of others
- suffer pain
- are killed.

In the past, there were many gruesome punishments waiting for anyone who dared to do even a small crime.

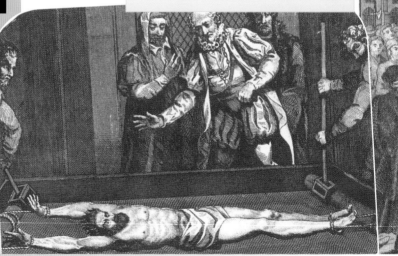

Word bank **penalty** punishment given for breaking a rule

Pain

History has been full of screams from people being punished. They were once put to death for crimes we no longer think are serious. Chopping down a tree could once lead to having your head chopped off!

The fear of being punished was meant to make people obey the law. It did not always work. It still does not! Criminals continue to get punished. Why?

- To make them think twice about breaking the law again.
- To be an example to other people, to stop them from becoming criminals.
- To pay criminals back for harming people.

Burning people to death in public was a warning to others to obey the laws.

Find out later...

What pain could you expect if you upset the Church?

What pain could you expect if you were a witch?

What pain could you expect if you told a lie in court?

Tough times

Putting people to death for doing wrong has been happening for a long time. Nearly 4,000 years ago the death penalty was used in Babylon (where Iraq is now) for 25 different crimes.

A punishment in China thousands of years ago was "death by a thousand cuts". So many cuts were made to the body that victims would "feel themselves die".

When leaders have too much power, they can punish whomever they like, for any reason. Through history there have been cruel leaders who have given all sorts of punishments.

Some leaders used **torture** to make prisoners talk and tell secrets. Sometimes it was just to make them suffer for something they had said or done. Cruel leaders have used pain and punishment to:
- give them a sense of power
- control anyone who argues or disagrees
- show hatred of anyone who is different or special
- make people pay up ... just to stop the pain
- change someone's ideas or behaviour
- warn others – if they do not obey, watch out!
- get **revenge**.

Romans would ⋯⋮ often throw criminals to their death off a cliff.

Word bank   crucifixion   putting to death by nailing the hands and feet to a cross

Early days

The Romans, 2,000 years ago, had many cruel leaders. The Emperor Nero used to set wild dogs or lions on people he did not like. In fact, the Romans put many criminals to death. Public **crucifixion**, drowning at sea, or being buried alive was done to show others what would happen if anyone dared to break the law.

The Greeks

Over 400 years before Nero, Greek leaders punished teachers who taught "the wrong things". The famous teacher Socrates taught young people to question ideas about the Greek gods. For this he was found **guilty** of **corrupting** the young. He had to drink poison, and died.

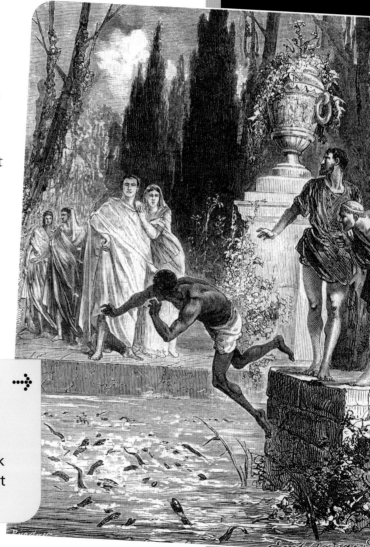

This picture shows a slave who had broken a cup. His master had him thrown into a tank of hungry eels that ate him alive.

revenge   getting even
torture   causing someone great pain

The Aztecs

The Aztec people lived in Mexico from around the 1100s up until the 1500s. They had some harsh punishments for anyone who broke their laws. Criminals were taken to a court where a group of judges would decide the punishment to be given to those found **guilty**. In many cases, it could mean death or being sold as a slave.

Here are the punishments given by Aztecs for some crimes:

Crime	Punishment
Cutting down a living tree	Death
Handling stolen property	Sold as a slave
Moving a field boundary	Death
Being drunk	Head shaved and house destroyed

Aztec death sentences could be by drowning, stoning, skinning alive, or being strangled.

Incas

Between 1200 and 1535, the Inca people lived in part of South America, including Peru and Chile. They were fierce fighters and also had tough punishments.

A thief or murderer could expect to die in one of many different ways. They could:

- be thrown off a cliff
- have their hands cut off or eyes cut out
- be hung up to starve to death
- have their head cut off
- be stoned to death
- be thrown into a pit of wild animals.

The bad news was, these punishments were not just for really serious crimes. If you told more than two lies … the third time would be your last!

An illustration of a hanging in England, from around 900ce.

The rope

The death **penalty** has been used in Europe for hundreds of years to punish criminals and to warn others against committing crime. A very common type of death penalty was hanging. Usually a rope was placed around the neck and the person would be hanged until they died.

Torture

All kinds of painful ways to punish people were used from 1,000 years ago. Often special instruments were made – just for giving pain.

Obey or else

The Roman Catholic Church was very powerful in Europe 800 years ago. People had to obey all its rules. If anyone dared to say anything against the Catholic Church, it could mean death – a painful one. The pain was to make someone **confess** to being sinful and to say sorry. Disagreeing with the teaching of the Church was called **heresy**. It was seen as a very serious crime. Anyone found guilty was likely to be burned to death.

People in the Middle Ages believed in all kinds of things, including dragons!

Word bank   confess   own up to doing something wrong
heresy   having opposite beliefs to those of a church

You'll be sorry

Spain was not the place to be if you were not a good Roman Catholic. For over 300 years from the late 1400s, you could be killed for speaking out against the **pope**. Anyone could report you and you would be taken off for **torture**.

One method of torture could mean being tied on to a wheel. The wheel was turned so you would go upside down. Your mouth would be gagged as water was poured down your nose. At the same time ropes tied around your body would be tightened. It would feel like your whole body was about to burst.
You would confess to anything!

Sometimes fire was used with the torture wheel, instead of water.

No hope

One way that **priests** thought they could tell if people were guilty of heresy was to tie them up and throw them into a river (shown above). If they floated, they were guilty and would be punished. If they sank and drowned, they would not be guilty … just dead!

Braveheart

The crime of **treason** is trying to overthrow the leader or government of your own country. The punishment for this crime has always been painful.

William Wallace was a Scottish hero who led his country in battles against the English. In 1305 English soldiers **arrested** him and led him through the streets of London. Crowds jeered and pelted him with rotten food.

Wallace was found **guilty** of treason. That meant a cruel public death. He was stripped, tied up behind two horses and dragged face down for 6 kilometres (4 miles). The worst was yet to come.

Jefferson Davis

Jefferson Davis (1808–1889), below, was president of the southern Confederate States of America during the American **Civil War**. When the Confederates lost the war, Davis was captured. He was imprisoned in Virginia in 1865 and charged with treason. After being held without trial for two years, the charge was dropped and he was released.

Word bank   arrested   to be taken in for questioning about a crime

Cut up

Like others found guilty of treason, William Wallace was hanged, drawn, and quartered. That meant being hung by the neck until half dead. While still alive, his body was cut open and his insides were pulled out (drawn). They were cooked in front of him while he was still alive. Only after he had suffered all this, his head was cut off. His body was cut into four (quartered) and each part was buried in different parts of the country. His head was stuck on a pole on London Bridge as a warning to others.

French treason

Joan of Arc was a young French woman who led soldiers in a war against England in the 1420s. She believed she was being led by God to do this. Joan was captured by the English and they accused her of committing treason against God. She was burned at the stake in 1431.

This is a painting of William Wallace being dragged through London. In reality he was stripped naked and dragged face down.

treason   crime against a leader or government

To torture someone is to cause them great pain and agony. The Latin word tortura means "twist". From this comes the word "distort", which means to twist out of normal shape. That was just what happened to many bodies as they were punished in the past.

The rack

The Tower of London was a prison in the Middle Ages. It was also a place of **torture**. Today, visitors can see many of the instruments that were used to punish prisoners hundreds of years ago.

The **rack** was a painful stretching machine that was probably invented by the ancient Greeks 2,000 years ago. From the 1400s, the Tower of London heard the rack creaking and groaning as it stretched prisoners into **confessing**. After just a few minutes of being pulled and twisted, a prisoner would be screaming in agony.

Being stretched on the rack made prisoners confess to anything.

Word bank   **pincers**   tool with two handles and two jaws that are used to grip things

Broken bodies

If you were a prisoner facing the rack, first you would be tied on to the machine. As the rack began to move it would stretch your whole body. It would pull your arms and legs from their sockets. Your bones would break one by one. The ropes tied round your ankles and wrists would pull tighter and tighter. They would cut deep into your flesh.

Screaming in agony, many prisoners ended up confessing to almost anything. Even if they were totally **innocent**, they might admit to any crime just to stop the pain.

Making sure

In Europe in the 1500s the Catholic Church used the rack to make people confess to **heresy**. Victims were sometimes stretched very slowly for days. Bodies could stretch by as much as 30 centimetres (12 inches). If that did not make someone confess, red-hot **pincers** could be used to tear off tongues, ears, and noses.

The Tower of London once echoed with the screams of prisoners.

rack   instrument of torture on which the whole body is stretched

From the 1500s more and more people began to travel further away from home. This helped the spread of ideas, but also the spread of crime.

Strict

Leaders in charge of some countries felt they had to be strict in order to keep their people under control. So they had to show they could be tough. They did this with strict laws and also with terrible punishments. They used **torture** to make people **confess** to any plots against them. Some of the instruments of torture used at this time were:

- thumbscrews – that slowly twisted and crushed both thumbs
- head crusher – that slowly cracked the skull like a nut.

Cooked to death

From 1491 to 1547 King Henry VIII ruled England. He brought in new, cruel punishments for criminals. About 72,000 people were put to death while he was king. Some of those were boiled alive.

The Iron Maiden ⤏ was an instrument of torture, full of spikes.

Word bank **branding iron** tool once used to burn a mark on criminals as a sign of their crime

Iron Maiden

Imagine being put inside an iron box. As the lid shuts, spikes in it stab your body. This instrument of punishment was called an Iron Maiden. It was used in Germany in the 1500s to hurt people, rather than kill them. But if people were left long enough, they would die.

A story from 1515 told that a German **forger** of coins was put inside an Iron Maiden. As the lid was slowly shut, spikes poked his body just enough to cause terrible pain, but not enough to kill him. He was left inside to think about his crime. He lived for two days in this agony.

Marked for life

Just as in Europe, criminals in the United States faced some scary punishments. In the 1600s **branding irons** sizzled in places such as Maryland. Letters were burned on criminals' cheeks, hands, or foreheads: T for thief, F for forger, B for burglar.

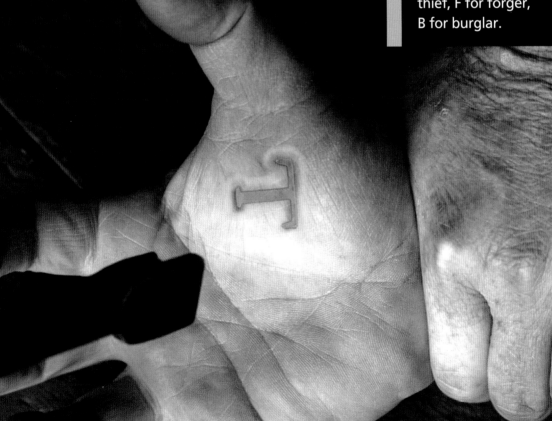

forger   someone who makes a copy of something and pretends it is the real thing

Five hundred years ago anyone could be arrested as a witch. People were at risk if they:

- looked unusual
- had a mental illness
- talked to their pets
- lived alone
- were old or disabled.

Witch hunts and witch finders

When people did not know what caused things such as thunder or disease, they lived in fear. A skin rash, for example, was often seen as a **curse** – when it was more likely due to fleas. People blamed witches for putting curses on people and for causing disease or bad weather.

Being a witch in the 1600s was a major crime. Thousands of people across Europe and the United States were killed for being witches. In the UK the punishment was usually to be burned. In the United States, witches were mostly hanged. Either way, **innocent** people were cruelly killed.

People accused of being witches were often lowered into a river on a special seat called a ducking stool.

Word bank   accuse   charge with a crime

Salem witches

Witches were said to be at work in Salem, United States, in the 1690s after two women became ill. Their doctor said the only thing to explain their illness was a curse. This began a panic. Men and women were **accused** of being witches and were **arrested**. Many went to prison and nineteen people were hanged.

In 1692, 80-year-old Giles Corey was accused of witchcraft. He was punished and forced to admit that he made curses – by being pressed to death under a heavy weight. The story says that as he was dying his tongue poked out and the sheriff simply poked it back in with his cane.

An illustration of a witch trial in Salem.

Hunting for witches

Matthew Hopkins was the "Witchfinder General" in England in the 1600s. He was paid for each of the 400 people he got hanged. Witches were said to have a "mark of the devil" on their body. Anyone with a spot or wart that did not bleed when Hopkins pricked them with a needle was arrested as a witch. He often cheated!

curse   wish for harm or injury to come to someone

Off with the head

For hundreds of years, people have been punished for crimes by having their heads cut off. This was often done in front of a cheering crowd. Beheading with a sword or axe was easy, cheap, and quick.

Because the Greeks and Romans used beheading, it became common across Europe and Asia. In fact, it is still used today in Saudi Arabia, Yemen, and Iran.

For the chop

Beheading was a punishment used for important people such as kings and queens. They would often be blindfolded and led to a wooden block (above) where they placed their neck. As the axe came down with a thud it was thought to cause no pain. A crowd clapped as the head rolled. Straw was put down to soak up all the blood.

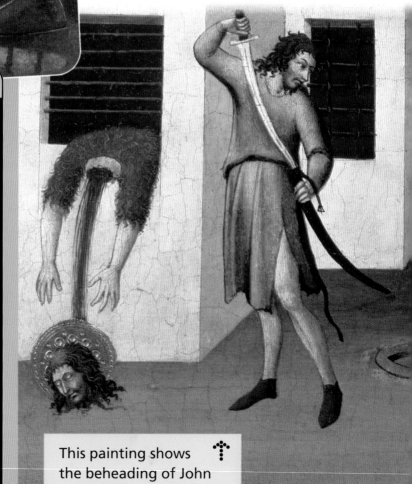

This painting shows the beheading of John the Baptist in Jordan.

A messy end

Queen Elizabeth I of England was worried that Mary Queen of Scots was a threat to her. So, she ordered that Mary be **executed** by having her head cut off! In 1587 Mary had to climb the steps to a platform, kneel down, and put her neck on to a block. She paid the axeman to do a good job. He failed.

The axe swung down – and missed! The blade sliced the side of Mary's neck and she cried out. The second chop cut the back of her neck, but not all the way through. He had to chop yet again. Only then did her head fall off.

Beheading

- Britain used beheading from 1076 up to 1747.
- Beheading was still used in Norway until 1905, in Sweden up to 1903, and in Denmark and Holland up to 1870.
- Hanging took over from beheading in Japan at the end of the 1800s.

Find out how France had another way of removing heads on page 28!

Bad hair day

The story of Mary Queen of Scots and her axeman had a final twist. When he tried to pick up her head to show everyone, he grabbed her hair – which was a wig. The head fell out of the wig and bounced across the floor.

An illustration of Mary Queen of Scots with her neck on the block.

Stocks were wooden frames that held people by the wrists or feet. In China prisoners in stocks would be **tortured**. The soles of their feet were covered with itching powder or their toenails were pulled out.

Pillories (below) locked the head as well. They were used in Asia and Europe for at least 1,000 years until the 1800s.

Suffering and shame

A **pillory** was a wooden frame that locked around a criminal's hands and head. He or she was then stuck in a public place to be laughed at. This could be for many days in all weathers. Not only was this punishment uncomfortable and painful, but it was also meant to bring shame to the criminal. It was used to punish even minor crimes such as cheating at cards, selling poor goods, or even swearing.

Crowds would shout insults and spit, but far worse could happen. They would sometimes throw rotten eggs, mouldy food, and dung. Some people even threw stones and rocks – which could kill the criminal.

Word bank   **pillory**   wooden frame with holes in which the head and hands can be locked

Boston crime records

Records from Boston show the kinds of crime that were punished in the United States in the 1600s. Men were tied to a post and whipped in public for:

- stealing a loaf of bread
- shooting a bird on a Sunday (Sundays were to be set aside for church, so having fun or doing work would be punished)
- swearing (people could also have holes cut through their tongue for this).

"In State Street was the pillory with four fellows fastened by the head and hands. The crowd pelted them with rotten eggs and every **repulsive** kind of garbage."

(Samuel Breck of Boston, United States, in the 1700s)

1600s crimes

In Boston in 1643, Roger Scott was whipped for "sleeping on the Lord's Day" and for "striking the person who waked him from his Godless **slumber**."

In 1648 in St Mary's City, Maryland, John Goneere told a lie in court so was sentenced to be "nailed by both ears to the pillory (like the image above) and whipped twenty good lashes."

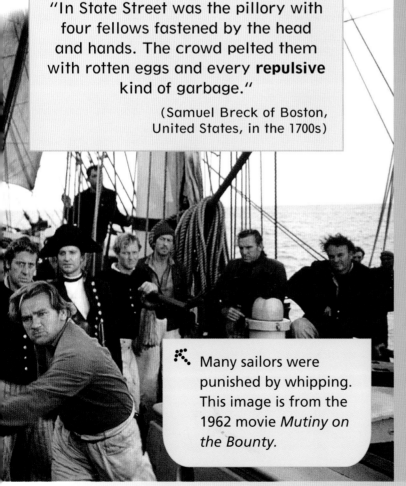

Many sailors were punished by whipping. This image is from the 1962 movie *Mutiny on the Bounty*.

repulsive   revolting and disgusting
slumber   sleep

23

Hanging

Hanging could be a slow and cruel death. Crowds would gather at the **gallows** to watch criminals twist in agony as the rope strangled them. In the last 400 years, over 13,000 criminals were hanged in the United States. About 500 of those were women. About 270 were children.

Jane Champion was the first woman to be hanged in the United States. She hanged in 1632 in Virginia for an unknown crime. Hannah Ocuish, aged 12 years, was the youngest girl hanged. She was found guilty of murder in 1786. George Stinney was 14 when he was hanged in South Carolina in 1944 for murdering an 11-year-old girl.

Death Penalty

The death **penalty** was first used in the United States when Daniel Frank was hanged in Virginia in 1622 for stealing cattle. Hanging was the main type of **capital punishment** in the United States until the 1890s. The last public hanging in the United States was in Kentucky in 1936.

Word bank   **capital punishment**   being killed as punishment for a crime

Choked to death

Prisoners arrived at the gallows in carts pulled by horses. Rowdy crowds cheered them on. The cart was backed under the gallows as prisoners stood at the end of the cart. The rope around their neck was tied up to a beam. The hangman pulled hoods over their faces. The horses were whipped, the cart jolted forwards and the prisoners swung on the end of the rope.

Prisoners would twist in agony for some minutes. After a while the hangman or the prisoners' families would pull on the prisoners' legs to speed up the death. After half an hour the bodies were cut down and claimed by the family.

Can you believe it?

Even after 1800, children were hanged in the UK. In 1801 a boy of thirteen was hanged for stealing a spoon. In 1808 two sisters aged seven and eleven were hanged at Lynn for a crime that was not recorded. As late as 1831 a boy of nine was hanged at Chelmsford for starting a fire.

This illustration shows a criminal being hanged in England in 1676. It sometimes took a while for the person to die.

gallows wooden structure from which criminals were hanged

1700s and 1800s

The world of the 1700s was very different from today. Many people thought of criminals as sinners who had to be made pure – by flames.

The stake

Tying people to a stake and burning them alive was done for hundreds of years across Europe. Thousands of people who had upset leaders or the Church were put to death in this way. People **accused** of witchcraft were chained to an iron stake. A pile of wood was lit under their feet. If they were lucky they were strangled first. If not, they died a cruel death.

New York City

Very few people were burned at the stake in the United States. In 1741, however, New York City burned thirteen men at the stake for plotting to burn down the city.

···▸ The Romans often burned several victims at the stake at once. This image is from the 1964 movie *The Fall of the Roman Empire*.

A painful end

In 1726 Catherine Hayes was found guilty of killing her husband in the UK.

> ❝ To strike terror in the crowd of so horrid a crime, the Sheriff did not strangle her first. She was fastened to the stake by an iron chain round her neck. This was pulled at last to kill her when she began to shriek so much. In about an hour's time she was just ashes. ❞

An illustration of a woman being burned at the stake in the 1700s.

Wax heads

Madame Tussaud (below) was a famous artist who made real-looking human heads from wax. She collected real heads that rolled from the guillotines in the 1790s to make plaster moulds of them. She displayed her models in shows. Her name is given to many waxwork museums today. There are Madame Tussaud waxwork museums in Las Vegas (opened 1999) and New York City (opened 2000).

The French way

In France in the 1700s rich people lived well, while many poor people starved. It all changed in 1789 when the poor people had enough and began a **revolt**. They attacked the rich people and punished them, even the king, Louis XVI. This became known as the French Revolution.

For ten years during the revolution thousands of people were put to death. From 1792 this was done using a new "beheading machine", called the **guillotine**. A rope pulled the blade of the guillotine up high where it was locked in place. The victim then rested his or her neck on the cold steel below … and waited as the crowd cheered.

Word bank **guillotine** machine for cutting off a person's head with a blade sliding between two posts

The chop

The guillotine's blade fell at great speed. It sliced through the neck and the victim's head dropped into a basket. A metal tray caught the spray of blood as the body rolled off the platform and into a coffin.

Death was quick. Even so, it was reported that the eyes and mouths of beheaded people sometimes moved for a while. It was thought the human brain could live for a few seconds after the blood supply was cut off. Maybe the last thing the victim saw was the inside of the basket coming closer...

Joseph Guillotin (1738–1814) **invented** the guillotine.

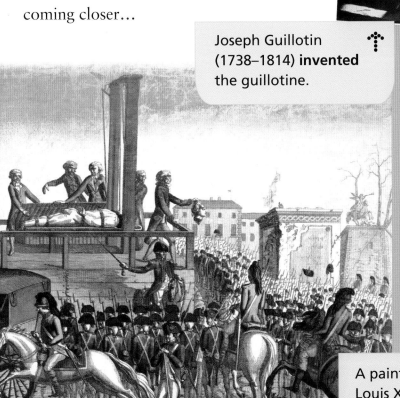

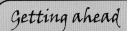
A painting of King Louis XVI being beheaded in 1793.

Getting ahead

When do you think the last person was beheaded with the guillotine in France?

- 1799
- 1844
- 1888
- 1933
- 1977

Turn to page 44 for the answer.

invent make or discover something for the first time
revolt rising up against leaders or government

29

Several convicts were sent off on a ship from Bristol, UK, heading for America. One of them cracked a rock into planks in the bottom of the ship to sink it, in the hope of escaping. But water filled the boat and no one escaped. Men were drowned and the rest were sent by the next ship to Virginia, America.

(Read's Weekly Journal, 12 October 1734)

Go away and don't come back

While the French were cutting off heads in the 1780s, ideas about punishment in the UK were changing. Many people felt it was time to stop putting criminals to death for minor crimes. Instead of being hanged, more criminals were sent to prison. But the prisons quickly filled up. The problem now was what to do with so many prisoners.

Before America fought and won **independence** from the UK in 1776, many British prisoners were sent there. Afterwards, America refused to take any more prisoners. The UK had to find somewhere else. Australia was the answer.

Convict ships were often in a bad state of repair. This is an illustration of the convict ship *Discovery*, 1828.

Word bank   **convict**   criminal serving a prison sentence
independence   freedom from outside control or support

Australia

From the 1780s, thousands of prisoners were sent to Australia from the UK. Taking fish from a pond or stealing a loaf of bread could result in such punishment – called **transportation**. It was not an easy punishment. The prison ships that took the **convicts** across the world were full of disease and rats. Many prisoners died on the eight-month journey. When they reached Australia life was very hard.

About 160,000 people were sent to Australia. Few were able to afford the journey back home again at the end of their sentence. Transportation was a really tough form of punishment. By 1870 it had stopped.

Keeping quiet

I have to keep a still tongue in my head. If I complain, I'd be hung at once. Or I'd get 100 lashes. Then I'd get sent to a place called Port Arthur Gaol to work in iron chains for 2 to 3 years…

(A letter sent by a convict doing **hard labour** in Australia to his father in 1835.)

Prisoners locked in cages in a convict ship on their way to Australia.

transportation   shipping of criminals across the world to prisons or for hard labour

No pain, no gain

The message had to be made clear in the late 1800s. Crime was wrong, and would be punished. Being made to suffer would make criminals think again about their "evil ways". Governments wanted to make sure they did not lose control in all the growing towns and cities. To stop people from turning to crime, prison had to be seen as a terrible place.

Prisons were used more and more to punish crime. But rather than keep prisoners locked up in cells, some prisons believed in making prisoners work. The idea grew that hard work was good for you. The more unpleasant the work, the better it must be!

Made to suffer

Punishments were made to make people suffer. Women in China in 1890 could be made to wear a heavy, square wooden collar for a while, sometimes up to a month! It let them move about, but it was extremely uncomfortable and inconvenient.

Word bank **chain gang** line of prisoners chained together and made to do heavy work

Make them work

Some countries made prisoners walk on **treadmills**. These were huge wheels that kept turning, rather like an exercise wheel for a hamster! The treadmills had no useful purpose other than keeping prisoners tired. This punishment was also meant to make them ache with pain. Then criminals would never want to break the law again. That was the idea.

Groups of prisoners chained together were taken out of prisons to work on the land, to build railways, or to break up rocks. It was very tiring work. These **chain gangs** were used a lot in the southern states of the United States – some until quite recently.

US prisoners in a chain gang at work in a quarry. They would be forced to work all day, often without a break.

treadmill   steps set around the rim of a big wheel that criminals had to walk on

The last 100 years

The 1900s brought many changes to the ways criminals were punished. Most countries gave up using the death **penalty** in the last 100 years. But the death penalty still exists in some places.

Death in the United States

The death penalty is still used in the United States. In some states the prisoner can choose not to be given a lethal injection, but to be hanged, **electrocuted**, or gassed. The number of death sentences in the United States has gone down from 71 in 2002, 65 in 2003, to 59 in 2004.

Electric chair

When it was first used in New York State in 1890, the electric chair was seen as **high tech**. Since then it has killed about 4,500 criminals in the United States. It is still used in a few places, although some states have banned the death penalty. Others have replaced the electric chair with a **lethal** injection. Is this a better way to kill serious criminals? Should they be killed at all?

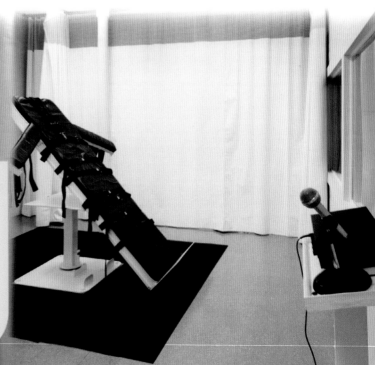

A lethal injection ···▸ chamber in Louisiana, United States. The prisoner is strapped to the chair before being injected with deadly poison.

Word bank   **electrocuted**   killed with a massive electric shock
high tech   using the very latest technology

Faulty wires

In Louisiana in 1946, the electric chair failed to kill Willie Francis. He was a 17-year-old muderer who cried out from the chair, "Stop it! Let me breathe!" He later said, "My mouth tasted like cold peanut butter. I felt a burning in my head and my left leg, and I jumped against the straps."

It turned out that the electric chair had not been set up properly. Francis was taken back to his cell and his lawyers argued that he should be let off. However, he was sent back to the electric chair the next year. This time it worked.

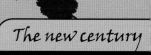

The new century

In 2003, there were at least 1,146 executions in 28 countries around the world. China, Iran, the United States, and Vietnam carried out 84 per cent of these known executions. Most of the prisoners were shot. Over 100 were hanged.

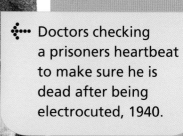
Doctors checking a prisoners heartbeat to make sure he is dead after being electrocuted, 1940.

The death penalty

Many people feel the death **penalty** might not be the best way to punish people. They ask three big questions:

- Does it really **deter** criminals? Does the fear of being put to death stop people committing crime?
- Is it "**civilized**" for a country to take life? Some criminals are very cruel, but should we kill them in return?
- Can we be 100 per cent sure that an **innocent** person will never be put to death?

Over half the countries in the world have answered "no" to these questions. Many have removed the death penalty in the last 100 years. Perhaps others will do the same soon.

The end of the death penalty

Place	Year
Michigan (first US state)	1846
Italy	1947
New Zealand	1961
UK	1973
Australia	1984
Kansas & New York State	2004

Beheading has 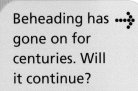 gone on for centuries. Will it continue?

Word bank   **civilized**   behaving with high standards and respect for others

No change

Not all countries have changed with the times. Some still use punishments that were used in the Middle Ages. Beheading is still a punishment for murder and other crimes in Saudi Arabia. Prisoners are taken to a public square or car park. With chained feet, they are led to a plastic sheet and made to kneel. They are blindfolded, with hands cuffed behind their back. An **executioner** raises a sword. With a sudden swipe he brings it down and cuts off the prisoner's head.

In the 1990s women were beheaded for the first time in Saudi Arabia. In 2003, 52 men and one woman were beheaded.

Firing squad

Some states in the United States used the firing squad to **execute** murderers. In 2004 Utah passed a law to ban the use of firing squads. That left only Idaho and Oklahoma where this punishment is **legal**.

A firing squad from the 1958 movie *Paths of Glory*.

executioner   person who carries out a death sentence

21st century

It might be hard to believe but even in the 21st century people are still punished in public. Some countries still make criminals feel pain. Parts of Nigeria in Africa have tough laws for thieves. If a thief is caught stealing, he or she can expect to have a hand cut off. Some other countries do the same.

In Sokoto, north Nigeria, a 30 year-old man paid the price for being a thief. In 2001 his right hand was cut off. This was punishment for stealing a goat. This was the third such punishment since eleven states in Nigeria brought in stricter laws for theft in 1999.

Is stealing something worth losing a hand over?

Do you know the difference?

Another term for the death penalty is **capital punishment**. One meaning of the word "capital" is "head". Capital punishment was used to describe: "losing the head".

One of the meanings for the word "corporal" is "body". Corporal punishment describes hurting the body. Corporal punishment was used a lot in schools to punish children in the last century.

Word bank   **corporal punishment**   being punished with pain to the body

Whipping

Saudi Arabia still believes **corporal punishment** is the best way to deal with thieves. In 2002 a court in Jeddah sentenced two car thieves. They had been caught driving a stolen car. One was given a sentence of 7 years in prison. That was after 1,680 lashes of the whip. His friend got 4 years and 600 lashes. The 1,680 lashes were given over 7 days. The second thief was lashed 15 times with 40 strokes each time. The judge said the two men were not given the same number of lashes because of the different number of crimes they had each committed before.

"I thought it would be fast but no, it was done one at a time ... I started counting and when it reached 40 I thought I could not make it ... I prayed so hard ... Soon it reached 60 ... I could not explain the pain."

(One of the car thieves who was whipped in Saudi Arabia, 2002.)

A lash with whips like these can leave terrible scars on the body.

New ways

- tags are fitted to the wrist or ankle (below)
- a monitoring box is fitted to a phone
- the tag constantly sends a signal to the box
- if the signal stops, an alarm goes off.

South Africa believes tagging will let out 30,000 prisoners from its overcrowded prisons.

For thousands of years criminals have been punished in many ways. Yet crime is still a big problem all around the world. So the big question is: Does punishment really work?

People once thought, "The more painful the punishment, the more likely it will stop crime." Were they right? Looking back, there is not much proof this was the case.

Countries today that use **capital** or **corporal punishment** still have crime. Do countries with the death **penalty** have fewer murders than countries without it? It would seem not. Some countries with the death penalty have far more murders than those without it. What do you think?

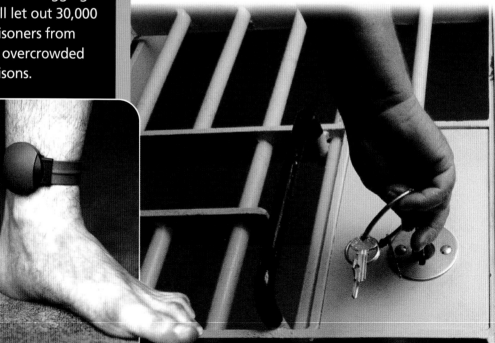

Word bank   supervise   keep a close check by watching someone closely

Easing the pain

For most criminals, loss of freedom is a real punishment. But prisons are crowded and expensive to run. So many countries now use other punishments for non-violent criminals:

- Tagging: a special **tag** fitted to the criminal sends an electrical signal to the police. It lets them know if the criminal is where he or she is allowed to be. That may mean the criminal having to stay at home.
- Day reporting centres: the criminal can live at home, but must go to classes each day – with all their movements being closely **supervised**.
- Community Service: the criminal must work for the local community, doing jobs such as tidying public parks. This earns back his or her freedom.

Meeting face to face can be very difficult for both the criminal and the victim.

Meeting

Some criminals agree to meet the victim of their crime. In a supervised place where the victim is safe they can say just what it was like to suffer from crime. It can be painful for the criminal to listen, but there have been many cases where this has helped both the victim and the criminal. It can even stop criminals committing crime again.

tag   something that is worn as identification

Progress?

Old-fashioned ideas

At one time children were made to behave by being beaten. Hard punishment was thought to make children honest and tough. Then they would never dream of committing a crime. Our ideas have changed since then! What do you think about such ways of raising children?

Today we can look back on the painful ways people once punished others. We have come a long way from the witch-hunts and **persecution** that terrified thousands. Most countries now allow free speech so that everyone can speak their minds without being thrown into boiling oil.

Most of us no longer think that pain is the answer for small crimes or for having different beliefs or ideas. We shudder at the thought of the **rack** twisting **confessions** from screaming prisoners. We no longer think prisons must be full of pain. But all of this was normal until less than 200 years ago … and still is in some places today.

42   *Word bank*   **persecution**   hunting down and treating people cruelly for their beliefs

Moving on

In most countries today, punishment fits the crime far better than it used to. No longer is chopping down a tree, for example, seen as an evil offence. Laws are much fairer now. They protect the public as well as **deter** criminals. Prisons now try to **reform** criminals in the hope of teaching them better ways to live.

People still have to fight for the rights of prisoners in some places. This is so they will be treated with respect rather than pain. It is also to stop **innocent** people from being punished, the way they often were in the past. A painful past that is best left far behind.

What next?

Each new age has to find ways to fight crime. Criminals will always be hiding in the shadows. So how will they be punished in the future? Many people believe that crime prevention is the answer. That means making crime even harder to commit in the first place.

People protesting against the death penalty, California, 2001.

reform   correct or improve someone's behaviour or habits

Find out more

Books
A Punishment to Fit the Crime?, A. Cooper (Franklin Watts, 2004)

Crime & Punishment Through Time, Ian Dawson (John Murray, 1999)

Life in Prison, Stanley Williams (SeaStar Books, 2001)

True Crime: Cops and Robbers, John Townsend (Raintree, 2005)

Using the Internet
Explore the Internet to find out more about crime through time. You can use a search engine, such as www.yahooligans.com, and type in keywords such as:

- Amnesty International
- capital punishment
- guillotine.

Search tips
There are billions of pages on the Internet so it can be difficult to find exactly what you are looking for.

These search tips will help you find websites more quickly:

- Know exactly what you want to find out about first.
- Use two to six keywords in a search, putting the most important words first.
- Be precise. Only use names of people, places, or things.

Getting ahead

Answer to the question on page 29:

- Hamida Djandoubi was the last person to be guillotined on 10 September 1977 in Marseilles, France.

- Djandoubi was **executed** for murder and **torture** of a girl. France ended the death **penalty** for all crimes in 1981.

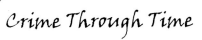

1215	England	Writing of the Magna Carta (Law of the Land).
1253	England	Parish constables start patrolling some areas, being paid by local residents.
1475	England	**Invention** of the muzzle-loading musket.
1539	England	First criminal court established at Old Bailey.
1718	England	Machine gun invented by James Puckle.
1789	United States	Constitution (Law) **ratified.**
1829	UK	Sir Robert Peel begins a proper police force with 1,000 uniformed police officers, based at Scotland Yard, London.
1830	United States	First revolver made by Samuel Colt.
1833	United States	First paid police force in the United States, based in Philadelphia.
1868	UK	Last public hanging in the UK.
1870	United States	Creation of Department of Justice.
1878	UK	Creation of Criminal Investigation Department.
1935	United States	Bureau of Investigations becomes the Federal Bureau of Investigations (FBI).
1936	United States	Last public hanging.
1987	UK	First use of DNA typing in solving crimes.

Glossary

accuse charge with a crime

arrested to be taken in for questioning about a crime

branding iron tool once used to burn a mark on criminals as a sign of their crime

capital punishment being killed as punishment for a crime

chain gang line of prisoners chained together and made to do heavy work

civilized behaving with high standards and respect for others

civil war when soldiers from the same country fight against each other

confess own up to doing something wrong

convict criminal serving a prison sentence

corporal punishment being punished with pain to the body

corrupt turn bad

crucifixion putting to death by nailing the hands and feet to a cross

curse wish for harm or injury to come to someone

deter put off or stop

electrocuted killed with a massive electric shock

execute put to death by law

executioner person who carries out a death sentence

forger someone who makes a copy of something and pretends it is the real thing

gallows wooden structure from which criminals were hanged

guillotine machine for cutting off a person's head with a blade sliding between two posts

guilty having done wrong

hard labour very hard physical work for little or no payment

heresy having opposite beliefs to those of a church

high tech using the very latest technology

independence freedom from outside control or support

innocent not guilty of a crime

invent make or discover something for the first time

legal allowed by law

lethal causing death

penalty punishment given for breaking a rule

persecution hunting down and treating people cruelly for their beliefs

pillory wooden frame with holes in which the head and hands can be locked

pincers tool with two handles and two jaws that are used to grip things

pope the leader of the Roman Catholic Church

priest someone in charge of a church

rack instrument of torture on which the whole body is stretched

ratified to be made official

reform correct or improve someone's behaviour or habits

repulsive revolting and disgusting

revenge getting even

revolt rising up against leaders or government

slumber sleep

superstition believing in unexplained powers, fear of the unknown, or trust in magic

supervise keep a close check by watching someone closely

tag something that is worn as identification

torture causing someone great pain

transportation shipping of criminals across the world to prisons or for hard labour

treadmill steps set around the rim of a big wheel that criminals had to walk on

treason crime against a leader or government

Index

Titles in the *A Painful History Of Crime* series include:

A Painful History of Crime
Crime Through Time

John Townsend

Hardback   1 844 21391 9

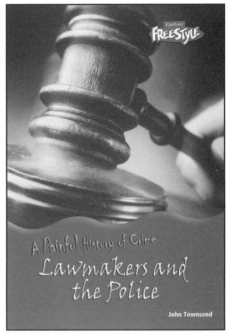

A Painful History of Crime
Lawmakers and the Police

John Townsend

Hardback   1 844 21390 0

A Painful History of Crime
Prisons and Prisoners

John Townsend

Hardback   1 844 21389 7

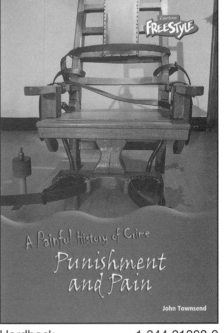

A Painful History of Crime
Punishment and Pain

John Townsend

Hardback   1 844 21388 9

Find out about other titles on our website www.raintreepublishers.co.uk